DATING INTROVERTED MAN & WOMAN

Proven Relationship Secrets for Dating Introverts

Robert Morgan

Contents

INTRODUCTION 4

    Being involved with an introvert 4

    The most effective method to date an introverted man 6

CHAPTER ONE 8

Introverts personality and relationship 8

    Should introverts date extroverts? 9

    Dating stuffs each introvert has to know 9

CHAPTER TWO 18

What to Know When Dating an Introvert 18

    What Is Introversion? 18

    Key Attributes 20

CHAPTER THREE 24

Tips on Effective Dating 24

CHAPTER FOUR 32

Techniques to communicate with introverted relationship 32

    What resounds most with you? 35

INTRODUCTION

Introverts regularly cut off up being in heartfelt friendships with an outgoing character in spite of the central contrast present in their demeanor.

Dating as an introvert is a troublesome errand for some individuals, and regardless of how much thoughtful people balance social butterflies out, the relationship is interesting. The inquiry emerges, can loners and outgoing individuals be seeing someone is glad and enduring?

At the point when it boils down to cherishing a introverts and extrovert relationship exhortation, there are a wide range of regions that you should know.

In any case, with the right sort of data, you can discover what an extrovert needs seeing someone. Likewise, to see how to have a relationship with a contemplative person and how to manage thoughtful people in a relationship, continue to peruse. This article is loaded with thoughtful person dating tips!

Being involved with an introvert

In case you are hitched to, sincerely intrigued and in any event, dating an introvert, there are several things you should know.

These dating tips for thoughtful person will help you in realizing what to do and what not to do.

1. Try not to think about it literally when they need time

The first introvert dating tip you should think about is that thoughtful people need some time alone and this steers clear of their accomplice. It doesn't imply that they are frantic or floating separated.

It simply implies that they need to re-energize themselves so they can return and be at the time altogether with their accomplice.

2. They needn't bother with casual conversation

When dating an introvert lady, you should realize that the general and little babbles can drive them insane. They don't care for it, nor do they see the value in it, and it before long becomes abnormal for them.

In any case, dating as a contemplative man or ladies, you should realize that inside and out talks are what grabs their eye. Significant points can make thoughtful people chatter endlessly with distinct fascination.

3. Try not to attempt to transform them

While adoring an introvert remember that they esteem your perspective the most.

In the event that you to such an extent as let them know that you need them to change their character or their propensities, they will stop themselves and push you away.

So all things considered, attempt to comprehend the distinction in their inclination and realize that they have their method of cherishing you. Keep in mind, introvert in adoration are the most mindful and delicate individuals, yet when they shut themselves out, they can be exceptionally mean and testing to coexist with.

The most effective method to date an introverted man

Regardless of whether you need to date a man or need to know how to date a thoughtful lady, there are sure things you should know. These things include:

-Once in a while contemplative people need a slight push to become social.

-After some time in a jam-packed spot or a party, a contemplative person will begin to remove themselves and retreat.

-Assuming you need to get your independent beau/sweetheart out of the house, then, at that point, you should design out your social schedule ahead of time.

-Introverts don't care for conversing with many individuals thus don't get mistaken for their quietness as them being uninterested.

-Ensure that you give additional consideration to their activities since they are not happy with shouting out.

-You can't change independent individual characters, so don't attempt.

CHAPTER ONE

Introverts personality and relationship

Many individuals can be excessively withdrawn for a relationship, and this term might confound any social butterfly when they initially hear it.

A relationship with an introvert can be a precarious yet the best relationship you can be in. To realize how to date as an introvert, you can peruse the contemplative person relationship exhortation referenced underneath and know more. This can likewise be useful in seeing how to date a withdrawn man.

Introverts perform best when in pair and with the one they love the most.

On the off chance that in an outgoing individual loner relationship, make a point to make arrangements that suit both of you.

Introverts show love with their activities rather than their words.

Like each and every other individual, introvert are particularly fit for discovering love. They are down to one side and straightforward individuals that like to invest energy with individuals they are agreeable around.

Should introverts date extroverts?

The response to this troublesome inquiry is yes; thoughtful people and social butterflies are especially fit for being seeing someone long as both the gatherings figure out how to think twice about. With the previously mentioned introverts' relationship guidance, an extroverts can live in a glad and durable relationship with no issue.

Utilize the previously mentioned focuses; know the response to questions like how to date as an introvert? How do introverts show love? Will loners experience passionate feelings for? Also, get them all replied.

Regardless of whether you need to know how to date a lady or a man, you have discovered your replies. Additionally, you currently realize what it resembles dating a contemplative lady or man.

Dating stuffs each introvert has to know

To each introvert, the demonstration of tracking down a huge different method doing something contrary to what you love most – blowing through another Netflix murder secret series in wool lined running pants. However, in the event that you really need a sidekick docs, it implies the feared Putting Yourself Out There.

Indeed, it may mean wasting a night in for a Kindling date who discusses speculation banking the entire evening and never ask you a solitary inquiry. However, fortunately, there are a few different ways to make the demonstration of going out somewhat to a lesser degree an overwhelming hellfire ride. The following are 11 hints for dating in case you're a reliable thoughtful person:

1. Ease the heat off yourself to be awesome.

-More from cosmopolitan

-Sex Master Responds to Bridgeton | Cosmopolitan

-Play Video

A date can time after time feel like an exhibition, or more awful, an assessment, which makes us freeze up, creator of How to Act naturally, Calm Your Internal Pundit and Transcend Social Uneasiness. It's much better to anticipate an abnormal quiet or two and a few jokes that crash and burn." Truly, you'd must be a narcissist or sociopath to not be a little hesitant or noticeably awkward on a first date. First dates should be the bubbly, marginally awkward inclination each-other-out stage. Embrace it!

2. Realize what sort of date draws out your chatty side.

It's presumably best that you have an overall measure of what you're doing on the date so you can recommend something different in case it's not your energy (like, say, a show). I think anything excessively boisterous and diverting is simply going to prompt you closing down additional, Teacher Emerita of Mental and Mind Studies of the College of Massachusetts, Amherst. Your best foot forward is truly exploiting your qualities, and it's by and large peaceful and intelligent.

Nonetheless, if taking a seat at a tranquil bar with an outsider and making discussion feels difficult to you, you can go the contrary course and pick a movement to do together. Some restless introverts depend on going to an occasion, similar to a perusing or a satire show, since it gives an underlying subject of conversation thereafter. Whatever it is, simply ensure it's something that will cause you to feel great.

3. Wear something comfortable and natural.

In the event that your everyday look is a sweater and pants, you'll likely need to forego proclamation lipstick and an open-back dress regardless of whether you think it appears to be more certain. In case you're zeroing in on how strange you feel, it just ups the tension.

It's equivalent to a new employee screening – you would prefer not to wear a fresh out of the plastic new outfit and not know whether it's excessively close or excessively short. Wear something you had great encounters with previously and have a decent outlook on – and is suitable for the event.

4. Prep somewhat ahead on convo themes.

In case you're extra stressed over running out of things to discuss, recommends a touch of pre-arranging. You can discover a tad about the individual early and have points that will not run into impasses.

Be genuine: in the event that you discovered this individual on an application, you presumably investigated their Instagram at any rate. No mischief in turning a portion of those climbing pics from seven weeks prior into first-date-question gold!

5. Ask 'indeed, and' questions.

Avoid shut finished inquiries questions that can be responded to in single word, similar to 'Where are you from?' or 'Do you have any kin? Think about the cardinal guideline of parody comedy: 'indeed, and.' Pay attention to whatever is being said, and afterward riff off of it." And in case you're the just one doing the legwork (it'll be quite self-evident in the event that they're giving you nothing to work with) – your date simply sucks and you can finish off your tab in harmony. Which carries me to:

6. Totally have an exit from the date in case need be.

In case of being burdened with the most noticeably terrible conversationalist (or only somebody with horrendous sentiments), you'll need a secure way out. "Nervousness is driven by vulnerability, so on the off chance that you have an adaptable leave plan, you'll feel more confident.

Also, in case you're anxious about feeling the strain to remain out truly late (regardless of whether the date is acceptable), you can design something between occasions, or during the day. "It's nice to make some positive memories you need it to be done. Assuming you go on a Saturday evening date, there's no obligation to what exactly occurs straightaway.

7. Get criticism if each date is a flop.

In the event that you've gone on a small bunch of dates and they've all been unnatural and excruciating to traverse, it very well may be a great idea to reexamine your own conduct on dates. "In case you're shaky with regards to your social abilities, you could get criticism from dear friends and discover how you're running over.

8. Sort out in the event that you have really have social tension, not simply introversion.

Inner-directedness is a character attribute and inclination – it doesn't consequently make you modest or off-kilter. On the off chance that conversing with anybody new oddities you out, regardless of whether it's pretty much every one of the things you bad-to-the-bone stan the most, you may be something beyond independent.

With social uneasiness, perhaps the greatest dread individuals have is meeting outsiders. In the event that you think you have a ton of fears that bunch together, it very well may be nice to search guiding and discover where these feelings of trepidation of meeting new individuals are coming from.

9. Trench the applications in case they're worrying you.

Thoughtful people can feel tremendous dating application weariness, particularly when they're caught in a pattern of swiping however never needing to really go on the date. In the event that you had several terrible encounters with applications, you will be significantly more apprehensive with regards to it. On the off chance that you don't care for an online application and you would prefer not to go out, it will make intense and put more squeeze on you.

So how would you meet individuals sans applications? There's investigating individuals at a party or joining a club, which likewise implies propelling yourself out of your usual range of familiarity (yet hello, basically you'll better know whether you network well with somebody off the bat). And afterward there's plunging into your organization. I thoroughly consider meeting individuals shared companions is a phenomenal technique. They're as of now verified, known substances, in addition to you have inherent shared traits to discuss. Regardless, being a shut-in doesn't mean applications are the most agreeable approach to date.

10. Think twice about going out with your partner once in a while.

Alright, so you discovered somebody who's incredible however needs to go out a little more regularly than you do. How would you think twice about? At times it merits directing your internal outgoing individual. We may not cherish stirring ourselves up to be 'on,' yet in the event that an individual or a reason is essential to you, it's totally awesome to propel yourself.

Also, there's one key component that is unique in relation to you being stuck at a local party alone: In case you're OK with your accomplice, they'll be there with you. You may discover it was more enjoyable than you suspected it would be.

This substance is imported from Facebook. You might have the option to track down a similar substance in another arrangement, or you might have the option to discover more data, at their site.

11. Yet additionally date somebody who gets you.

In the event that you need a little push to get out and have a good time, dating somebody more outgoing can achieve that," "Yet in case you're now truly hard on yourself and propel yourself savagely, it tends to be approving to date somebody who brazenly remains in." The primary concern is: this individual needs to acknowledge your settling, cover post devotee ways and never cause you to feel awful for them.

CHAPTER TWO

What to Know When Dating an Introvert

Where an extravert appreciates huge gatherings and going out, thoughtful people may favor a calm evening with dear companions. And keeping in mind that extraverts appreciate investing bunches of energy in friendly circumstances a loner will become exhausted and need time to re-energize after time spent in group environments. Thus, in case you're an extravert, a great deal of what a loner wills not sound good to you.

Also, it's extremely simple to confound their requirement for alone time as a pointer that they are simply not that into you. To hold you back from making bogus suspicions, it's significant that you realize what really matters to an introvert with regards to dating connections. This is what you need to know whether you're dating a thoughtful person.

What Is Introversion?

Before you can completely get dating a thoughtful person, you need to know what introspection is—and what it isn't. In general, introversion is a character quality where the individual spotlights more on inner sentiments instead of on outer wellsprings of incitement.

Ordinarily, individuals who are independent have a little gathering of dear friends, appreciate isolation, and discover huge gatherings or gatherings depleting on occasion. They likewise are exceptionally mindful, appreciate noticing individuals and circumstances, and are attracted to professions that encourage autonomy.

Note that introversion isn't exactly the same thing as being introverted, having social nervousness, or being modest.

With regards to inner-directedness, there likewise are various misinterpretations notwithstanding the way that thoughtful people make up around 33% to one-half of the world's population.1□□

Indeed, many thoughtful people report being misconstrued. At the point when they hush up, individuals frequently expect that something should be off-base or that they are irate or discouraged. Now and then individuals might even feel that they are distant or unapproachable.

All things being equal, most contemplative people might hush up, basically on the grounds that they don't want to be the focal point of consideration. They like to notice their current circumstance and individuals around them. What's more, they are generally more saved in what they share about themselves with others liking to become acquainted with somebody prior to opening up.

Furthermore, inner-directedness isn't a peculiarity or a shortcoming. Both introspection and extraversion have been distinguished in pretty much every types of the collective of animals including even organic product flies.

For example, there are organic product flies that will sit unobtrusively in one spot while others will meander around and investigate their environment. A few specialists accept that each approach gives a novel endurance technique and is imperative relying upon the circumstance. The equivalent is valid for people.

Here and there it is gainful to be an extravert and now and then it is useful to be an introvert. Both character attributes have worth and significance.

Understanding this reality is fundamental since it holds you back from expecting that one character attribute is liked over the other. All things being equal, simply acknowledge that extraverts and introvert are unique.

Key Attributes

With regards to recognizing introversion, it's significant not to mistake modesty for inner-directedness.

While the facts confirm that some thoughtful individuals may be modest, bashfulness isn't a characterizing normal for an introverted.

Indeed, there are a lot of withdrawn individuals who are cordial. Here are some key attributes that independent individuals frequently show:

Will in general be extremely attentive and measure things at a profound level

-Embrace isolation and need time alone

-Lean toward handling their contemplations inside instead of by working them out

-Decide to impart individual data to just a limited handful

-Incline toward composing, messaging, and different types of composed correspondence over talking

-Show less expressive feelings than their extraverted partners

-Re-energize their batteries by withdrawing and investing energy alone

-Become depleted and over-animated by huge gatherings of individuals

-Feel generally invigorated and animated in calm environments

-Have a little circle of dear companions instead of a huge circles

-Are extraordinary audience members and become acquainted with individuals on a profound level

-Set aside additional effort to comprehend thoughts prior to continuing on to new ones

-Want significant associations instead of casual discussion

The most ideal approach to decide if your partner is withdrawn is to just inquire. With regards to character and demeanor, individuals will in general have a very decent handle on what their identity is and what really matters to them.

Obviously, if your accomplice is uncertain, one approach to get more familiar with each other is to step through a character examination together or find out with regards to your main avenues for affection.

CHAPTER THREE

Tips on Effective Dating

On the off chance that you find that you are dating an introvert and you are an extravert or an ambivert—or regardless of whether you additionally are an introvert—it very well may be useful to realize how to move toward dating with an introvert.

From choosing the ideal date alternatives to giving them their space, dating an introvert doesn't need to be testing on the off chance that you know what your Partner may like. Here are a few hints to kick you off.

-Acknowledge Them

Too often, individuals attempt to change the individual they are dating as opposed to tolerating them for what their identity is. In case you're dating a thoughtful person, make an effort not to decide what their identity is or pressure them into being somebody else. All things considered, appreciate what your partner has to bring to the table.

Thoughtful people give the chance to their dating partner to dial back, ponder things, and become more reflective. In like manner, in case you're an extravert, you can give your partner the chance to attempt new things and meet new individuals.

The key is fail to remember all the social shame encompassing inner-directedness. The majority of it is exceptionally mistaken any way. Being thoughtful isn't a shortcoming nor does it imply that introvert don't care for individuals or that they are introverted.

Truth be told, many introverts do exceptionally extraverted things. They additionally like spending time with individuals. The thing that matters is that the thoughtful person will require time alone to re-energize subsequently and an extravert will not.

-Be a Protected Individual

Your independent accomplice is bound to open up and share their deepest feelings when they not just feel that they will be paid attention to yet additionally that you are a protected individual to impart individual subtleties to.

On the off chance that they feel like they need to continually rival you with regards to talking or then again on the off chance that you communicate everything, they will just tune in and not share a lot.

Ensure you are imparting that they are significant and significant by taking a portion of the concentration off yourself and really paying attention to what they need to say. With time, you might find that your contemplative accomplice is partner and insightful with an idiosyncratic funny bone.

-Make a Valid Association

Rather than zeroing in on doing whatever might be considered appropriate in a relationship like calling at the perfect opportunity, messaging reliably, and expressing the right things, center around making a significant association with your partner.

Truth be told, most loners want smart, intriguing discussions about something important to them.

In case you don't know what their inclinations are, ask them. Or then again in the event that you would like, share your interests or your objectives. Introverts need a psyche to-mind association where you share your internal world with them including what makes you tick. You likewise could have a go at asking your partner inquiries.

Many introverts will share their feelings and sentiments because of inquiries as opposed to chipping in data. Along these lines, be patient and ask your partner.

Simply make certain to really pay attention to what they need to say and try not to pressure them in case they are awkward noting or feel as they don't have a reply yet.

By being truly intrigued by their considerations and giving them space to share, you're more similar to get further more significant reactions.

-Pick Suitable Dates

Realizing that your introverted partner inclines toward more personal social occasions or calm nights, ensure you pick your dates likewise, particularly first and foremost.

For example, rather than hauling your partner to a work party time occasion where they will know nobody, welcome them to have espresso or supper with you. Take them to a film, go on a climb, or feed their scholarly side here and there.

In the wake of dating for a spell, your introvert partner will be bound to go to parties with you. Yet, in the first place, you might need to propose dates that will not be overpowering or unoriginal.

All things considered, what amount can you truly become more acquainted with somebody at a work party time when your consideration will be partitioned anyway?

-Search for Compromises

Realizing that introverts get fatigued at huge gatherings or occasions with loads of individuals, search for ways you can think twice about these circumstances. For example, possibly you concur early how long you will remain or maybe you drive independently with the goal that your partner can leave early in case they are feeling depleted.

Despite the fact that you might would rather that they brave the whole occasion with you, it is unjustifiable to put those requests on your contemplative accomplice. Other than proceeding to leave early is better compared to not going by any means.

Keep the lines of correspondence open as well, so you can figure out what turns out best for your relationship. A few couples concur that two times every month they will partner something the extravert appreciates and double a month they will partner something the introverts appreciates. In the meantime, different couples concoct a code word to utilize when they are at packed occasions.

Along these lines, the thoughtful partner can motion toward the other that they have arrived at their breaking point and they are prepared to leave. Having this word permits them to retire from the circumstance right on time without causing a ruckus or causing a great deal of to notice themselves.

However long you both work to regard each other's disparities and inclinations, you can have a solid relationship notwithstanding being perfect inverses.

-Become Familiar with Quietness

Do whatever it takes not to think about it literally if your withdrawn partner needs an ideal opportunity to de-pressurize and be distant from everyone else. Truth be told, it's normal for contemplative dating partners to rather not go through consistently together. This requirement for isolation is never about you actually and more with regards to their need to deal with the measure of incitement they have going on in their lives. Have confidence that once they feel revived and rejuvenated they will be available to hanging out.

Note that occasionally contemplative people would just prefer hush up about things—particularly in case something is pestering them. Not at all like extraverts who regularly measure their sentiments by discussing them, introverts like to handle these things inside and sort out how they are feeling and why prior to imparting it to someone else.

On the off chance that you find that your accomplice does this, be patient and give them the space they need. Ultimately, they will share what's at the forefront of their thoughts.

-Feature Your Partner's Qualities

Rather than zeroing in on what you don't comprehend about inner-directedness, center on what you appreciate about your partner's character type. For example, on the off chance that you respect the way that your partner is so open to being separated from everyone else without feeling desolate, bring up that to them. Or then again, maybe you like the way that they are delayed to talk however when they do they express profound and savvy viewpoints. Ensure they realize that.

Too often, individuals center on the negatives or the distinctions as a part of their character types and fail to focus on what pulled in them to each other in any case.

Therefore, be certain you are consistently reminding your introvert partner what you love most with regards to their character. Naturally, many introverts are adoring, merciful, and steady. In this way, there's a decent possibility that they additionally see numerous things in you that they respect too.

CHAPTER FOUR

Techniques to communicate with introverted relationship

Comprehend and embrace your requirement for alone time. To plainly communicate your requirement for alone an ideal opportunity to your partner, you should initially comprehend it yourself. The most ideal approach to begin understanding a component of your character and inclinations is to take an open, inquisitive, and tolerating position towards it. Anything you desire is extraordinary! Your inclinations, withdrawn or outgoing or whatever, are not off-base at all. This is basic, yet don't disparage its significance.

With a place of tolerating whatever we discover, how about we investigate how much alone time you need and what invigorates you most:

Do you require calm at specific occasions of day? Notice yourself as you travel through your timetable for the following not many days. When do you most hunger for uninterrupted alone time? In the mornings, evenings, nights? Previously or after specific exercises? What appears to invigorate you most during those occasions? In the event that you can distinguish when you most need alone time and what most reenergizes you, you can expand your re-energize minutes so you can get back to your partner new and glad.

Are there triggers that lead to requiring all the more alone time? When you have too much going on working, or when you go through an evening at a mixed drink party, do you require additional time alone? Notice the amount you need and when you need it so you can begin incorporating it into your daily schedule and re-energize consequently.

When you're worried or there's a contention, how long do you have to chill off? Do you require 60 minutes, two hours, or just a half-hour before you refocus with the main job or the contention you're attempting to determine with your accomplice? At the point when you know how much alone time you need, you can make the solicitation effortlessly. Your partner will be calm since they know you're not leaving; you're simply taking the time you need so you can have a decent conversation.

Do you have a specific beat of "on-seasons" and "slow times of year"? Large numbers of us pivot through patterns of friendliness and security. Do you have such a mood, and provided that this is true, what does it resemble? Is it occasional, where you're more dynamic in the mid-year and more private in the colder time of year? Is it week after week, where you're friendlier on Fridays and Saturdays and need the entire day Sunday alone? What is your special beat that makes you most joyful? Keep in mind, however much your accomplice might very much want to invest more energy with you, what they most need is to see you glad. In this way, if your dynamic alone mood fulfills you, sorting out your musicality and offering that information to your accomplice will satisfy them as well.

-Convey your requirement for alone time

How would you communicate your requirement for alone an ideal opportunity to your partner in a manner they can comprehend, feel calm with, and honor?

To begin with, make sure to comprehend and respect the reality you need this time. Recollect that when you require some investment you need, you are more joyful, not so much focused, but rather more drew in with your partner. That is the thing that makes it a mutual benefit. On the off chance that you remember that respecting your requirement for private time is useful for you both, your non-verbal communication and voice will normally be more easeful when you convey your necessities, and that will empower easefulness in your partner too.

A decent content may be, "Nectar, I've been doing some contemplating how I can best deal with myself so I can carry more satisfaction and presence to our relationship. I understood I truly need X time without help from anyone else to unwind and re-energize, particularly when X (season of day, triggers, conflicts, and seasons). At the point when I've had that time, I'm ready to be completely with you, which is the thing that I truly need. Does this sound affirm to you?"

-Understanding love languages

Quality Time: Significant and fun time spent together.

Uplifting statements: Praises, verbal consolation, and cherishing affirmation.

Gifts: Actual gifts, extraordinary or little.

Demonstrations of Administration: Supportive motions that make another's life simpler and more charming.

Actual Touch: Warmth through touch and actual closeness.

What resounds most with you?

You may all the more normally get love one way and all the more normally express it another way.

For instance, you may adore actual friendship when your accomplice starts, however you might be bound to communicate your affection through doing seemingly insignificant details around the house and making your accomplice's life simpler.

Impart how you express love

On the off chance that your accomplice has frequently said to you, "Nectar, I need us to hang out," or, "I truly like it when you offer me sweet commendations," you have an idea to your accomplice's normal love-getting language.